DEVELOPING YOUR People**Smart** SKILLS

A HANDBOOK SERIES

Asserting Your Needs

Mel Silberman, Ph.D.
with Freda Hansburg, Ph.D.

BK

BERRETT-KOEHLER COMMUNICATIONS, INC.

Berrett-Koehler Communications
450 Sansome Street, Suite 1200
San Francisco, CA 94111-3320
Tel: 415-288-0260   Fax: 415-362-2512
Website: www.bkconnection.com

Ordering Information

Please send orders to Berrett-Koehler Communications, P.O. Box 565, Williston, VT 05495. Or place your order by calling 800-929-2929, faxing 802-864-7626, or visiting www.bkconnection.com.

Special discounts are available on quantity purchases. For details, call 800-929-2929.See the back of this booklet for more information and an order form.

 Printed in the United States of America
on acid-free recycled paper.

ISBN 1-58376-160-8

Contents

Introduction

Check off the "people" activities below that apply to you:

- ☐ supervising employees
- ☐ parenting children (and one's parents)
- ☐ working on a team
- ☐ being in a committed relationship
- ☐ dealing with your boss
- ☐ participating in religious or community groups
- ☐ helping others understand how to do something
- ☐ coping as a consumer
- ☐ obtaining business
- ☐ interviewing others or being interviewed
- ☐ relating to doctors, nurses, and mental health professionals
- ☐ selling to a customer
- ☐ attending a party
- ☐ networking
- ☐ interacting with coworkers or classmates
- ☐ chatting on the Internet

Chances are you checked several of these items. It used to be said that some of us were in the business of working with people and some of us were in the business of working with facts, figures, and machinery. This distinction was probably never accurate, but its inaccuracy is now beyond dispute: Good people skills are a must for any job, including technical ones. Our lives at home also demand superior people skills as we try to juggle new roles and new living conditions. The people business is no longer the domain of the few. It includes you and everyone you know.

The twenty-first century will feature a rapidly changing and highly interrelated world. You will probably accomplish very little on your own, but with other people you may be able to accomplish a lot. Increasingly, success will depend on being people smart.

Ask the person on the street what it means to be people smart, and you may get an answer such as, "Oh, that's a person who is really a smooth operator . . . a person who knows how to get others to join his side." A second person might answer, "someone who is personable, friendly, fun to be with." While few people would complain about having those two attributes, they represent a very limited view of what it means to be gifted with people. Being people smart is a multifaceted intelligence, not limited to your political skills or your social graces but including a wide range of interpersonal abilities. One of them is asserting your needs.

In order to be people smart, you've got to be your own person. You have to have limits and you have to establish those limits. If you try to be all things to all people, you'll wind up disappointing them. You also need to be straightforward with your wishes. Hinting at what you need from others only leads to disappointment and frustration. Once that happens, you often become angry at others and lose the confidence you need to be at your best.

In *Asserting Your Needs*, you will find a five-step process for boosting this vital skill that is realistic and doable.

1. **You've got to SEE IT.** From the start, you must be honest with yourself and take stock of your strengths and weaknesses. To assist you with this process, we will provide you with a short survey that assesses your current ability level in asserting your needs. We urge you to rely not just on your own perceptions. Find the courage to ask others how they see you as well. Taking an honest look at yourself is the critical first step along the road to self-improvement.

2. **You've got to WANT IT.** Since changing long-standing habits won't come easily, you have to pay special attention to motivation. You are more likely to be motivated if you are aware of when and where you need the skill the most. To help you make this connection, we will provide you with a list of situations where you might find the skill in question to be particularly relevant in your life at the moment. Choose a situation or two in which you want to excel and focus on them.

3. **You've got to LEARN IT.** Those who are people smart do certain things very well. Become familiar with the skills possessed by people who assert their needs. While you don't need a whole course in this area to make some changes, it is important to acquire a few basics. Even if you are familiar with this material, we urge you to review it.

4. **You've got to TRY IT.** Reading about what others do well will not suffice—you must do it yourself. We will encourage you to conduct an "experiment in change." These experiments will allow you to try on a small change in behavior for size. You will test your wings and may find the initial success necessary to sustain further practice.

5. You've got to LIVE IT. One of the reasons that changes don't last is that after people get pumped up about doing something, they try to make it on sheer inspiration and willpower. They may make some headway but then quickly relapse. Real change comes only by overcoming obstacles that are in the way in our daily life. We will help you to confront *your* difficulties with asserting your needs. This skill may be difficult for you for reasons that are different than for someone else. If you face the reasons the skill is difficult for *you*, you will be more likely to incorporate the skill into your life.

If you think about it, these five steps apply to any area of self-improvement. For example, assume you are overweight. You might begin by taking a good look at yourself in the mirror and weighing yourself in order to **see it**. Even if you admit it to yourself, you really have to **want** to do something about it—especially if you love to eat. Therefore, it may prove necessary to increase your motivation by thinking about specific situations in which you want to enjoy the benefits of being lighter. Next, you might find it helpful to **learn** about the latest diets, ways to lose calories through exercise, and psychological tips to modify your eating behavior. When you decide to **try** something different, it will feel like an "experiment in change." If the experiment is successful, you may be able to build the approach you have been employing into your lifestyle. You will start to **live** it. Along the way, there will be plenty of obstacles to identify and find ways to overcome. If you do, the weight lost will stay off.

These five steps—*see it, want it, learn it, try it*, and *live it*—are especially important when you are seeking changes in your interpersonal effectiveness. You cannot develop your people smarts merely by osmosis.

Asserting Your Needs

Since people cannot read minds, you must tell them what you want.

—Patricia Jakubowski

You can't be all things to all people. If you try, you'll wind up disappointing them. That's because others will come to expect too much from you, and you're bound to fail from time to time.

We all have limits, even those among us who are "superhuman." And that is healthy. There are some things you shouldn't do for others, either because they need to do it for themselves or because it will rob you of your ability to care for yourself and for those who really need your help.

Besides having healthy limits, you also need to speak up so others know what they are. Holding back what you need from others only leads to frustration. Once that happens, you may become angry at others and lose the calm and confidence you need to be at your best:

Don is a people pleaser. He doesn't like disapproval and organizes his day around doing what will be popular with others. At work, Don lives by the motto, "You won't rock the boat if you follow the waves." He watches for clues and listens for statements about what others want and makes sure he's on the popular side. Being agreeable and willing to comply, he stays afloat but goes largely unnoticed when new opportunities arise. If you asked Don if his needs were being met, he would probably say they were. Resentment builds up slowly in him, but it begins to surface with sarcasm and erupts on occasion with uncontrollable anger.

Compare Don to Hank.

Hank is a devoted father and a supportive manager of people. Yet he knows that if he stretches himself too far, he'll lose his perspective and inner balance, so he lets people know when he has reached his limit of giving. You don't feel intimidated by Hank's assertiveness, but you do get the message that he's his own person —kind of like most cats we've had. Hank respects other people's needs as he respects his own. When you want something from Hank, he's more than willing most of the time. He also anticipates what you may need from him and provides it even before you ask for it. But if he can't fulfill a request, or just doesn't want to, he says, "I'm sorry I can't right now," or "I have to decline." He adds just enough explanation so that you know why. Consequently, you admire his directness and still feel that he's a nice guy.

See It
How Assertive Are You?

What sort of feedback have others given you about the way you assert yourself? If you asked friends or coworkers, would those people know what you wanted from them and what you would be willing to do for them? Who are you more like: Don or Hank?

Ask others for feedback. Pick someone you're comfortable with and say to the person: "I'm curious about something. Do you think I assert myself enough (or too much)? How do you see me?" Ask the person to share with you some specific information about how you come across and what you might try to improve. Make notes of what the person tells you. After you've worked on improving yourself, you may want to go back to the person, remind her of her feedback and ask whether she thinks you've made progress.

If you'd like to try rating your own current skill level, you can complete the following survey. (You might ask others to fill it out about you as well.) Think honestly about your own day-to-day actions at home, at work, with friends. Then rate yourself on the ten behaviors below:

Asserting Your Needs

(4–Effective   3–Good   2–Fair   1–Poor)

_____ 1. I keep calm and remain confident when I get opposition.

_____ 2. I explain my needs briefly and without defensiveness.

_____ 3. I don't let others pressure or rush me.

_____ 4. I am firm when I need to be.

_____ 5. I make good eye contact when confronting others.

_____ 6. I can say no with grace and tact.

_____ 7. I persist until important matters are worked out to my satisfaction.

_____ 8. I am decisive about what I will do or not do for others.

_____ 9. I stay focused on my goals.

_____ 10. I am not afraid to hear the other person's side.

_____ TOTAL

When you have rated your skill level on each of the items, total your score and compare it to the ranges below:

- 30-40: You see yourself as having strong, effective assertion skills and you use them consistently.
- 20-30: You believe you make some effort to assert yourself effectively, but see room for improvement.
- 10-20: You know you're in trouble, but at least you're willing to admit it!

Now that you've taken stock of how assertive you are, let's examine situations in which you want to improve.

Want It
Motivating Yourself to Become More Assertive

Think about when being more assertive would get your needs met. With whom do you want to be assertive? When? Do any of these situations apply to you?

On the job:

- ☐ Getting too much work from your boss.
- ☐ Wishing for more praise or appreciation from others.
- ☐ Dealing with colleagues who want to schedule a meeting time that is inconvenient.
- ☐ Getting repeated tongue-lashings from a coworker.
- ☐ Being sexually harassed.
- ☐ Unwanted overtime and unwelcome business travel.
- ☐ Being pestered by sales calls.
- ☐ Being visited by a coworker too often.

☐ Wanting your budget increased.

☐ Someone talking about you behind your back.

☐ Turning down a subordinate's request for reassignment.

☐ Receiving slow service from a supplier.

On the home front:

☐ Not receiving enough help with chores.

☐ Restricting TV viewing or computer usage.

☐ Requesting quality time with your partner.

☐ Demanding privacy.

☐ Coping with interfering parents.

☐ Expecting communication from your teenager.

☐ Being treated with disrespect by teachers, doctors, and others.

☐ Saying no to a charitable contribution.

☐ Feeling harassed by family members who want you to visit them.

☐ Arguing about attending religious services.

☐ Refereeing sibling disputes.

We hope these examples prompt you to pinpoint circumstances of your own where assertive communication could pay off for you.

Learn It
Three Ways to Become More Assertive

People become assertive by **being decisive**, by **remaining calm and confident**, and by **being persistent**. They are clear to themselves and to others about where they stand. They stay relaxed and self-assured as they express their needs and wishes. And they obtain what they need by sticking to their guns. By looking at each of these skills in more detail, you will get a better idea of what they involve and how to use them as your building blocks.

1. Being Decisive

Non-assertive people are fuzzy about both what they will do *for* others and what they want *from* others. They often operate by the seat of their pants, rarely thinking about how they feel and what they need. If a situation arises that they've been in many times before, they face it with fresh apprehension rather than with the security of knowing how they want to react. It's far better to be in the driver's seat, anticipating problems and being prepared.

How clear are you about such matters as:

- rules about your children's bedtime?

- requests to stop what you're doing and assist others?

- keeping within a budget?

- employee tardiness?

- the use of your car?

- last minute assignments?

- seeking and receiving affection?

- the amount of time you require to do a job?

- compensation for your services?

- the whereabouts of your child?

- telemarketing calls?

- noise and other distractions?

- returning unsatisfactory work or service?

- off-color humor?

Needless to say, we could list hundreds of issues! Little wonder that one might become confused and uncertain with others, but indecisiveness can carry a high price:

> *Lisa complained that her twelve-year-old daughter Dawn*
> *was constantly on the phone. "It's really very stupid,"*
> *Lisa told me. "She and her friends call each other as*
> *soon as they get home from school." When asked what*
> *she wanted of Dawn, Lisa retorted: "To stay off the*
> *phone!" Lisa was then asked to clarify her position:*
> *When could Dawn use the phone? How long per call?*
> *Under what conditions would Lisa allow a separate*
> *phone line? It took time for Lisa to decide how she*
> *wanted to answer these questions, but once she did, Lisa*
> *realized how unclear she had been and was eager to tell*
> *Dawn the new telephone rules.*

We are not suggesting that merely deciding what you want will automatically lead to *getting* what you want. Naturally, resistance can occur to even the most carefully thought-out requests. However, when you know what you want, you have taken a long stride toward obtaining it. As it is often said, "The more you know where you are going, the easier it is to get there."

There are three important steps in being decisive: *separate needs from wishes*, *take a stand*, and *communicate your position*.

Separate Needs from Wishes

Most of us wish for lots of things, but we don't need them all. Interpersonally intelligent people know the difference between needs and wishes. They ask themselves, "Is this something important? Do I really care about this matter?" Consequently, the weight of concerns they carry is light. By contrast, other people get bogged down with lower priorities. They give equal importance to every-thing that crosses their path. Their load is heavy.

Make a list of things other people do that get you upset. Think about your boss, your employees, your partner, your family, and even your neighbors.

Things People Do That Get Me Upset

I don't like it when: _____

_____

_____

_____

_____

_____

_____

_____

_____

_____

Now, review each item and ask yourself, "Is this something I must deal with now, or can it wait?" For example, imagine someone list-ing, "I don't like it when my assistant sometimes treats people as if he's annoyed to answer their questions." The question this boss must ask is whether this is a problem that should be addressed now or not. There might be more pressing priorities. You will be more successful asserting your needs if you let go of low-priority items, and concentrate your energy on those that remain. This fact is especially true for people who get easily upset at others.

A good way to assess each "I don't like" statement is to ask the following question: *Do I really want to press this matter at this time?* When doing this exercise, Jesse wrote the following:

"I don't like it when I'm asked to start a project and just as I'm getting into it, I'm pulled off into another assignment."

An interviewer then asked: *Do you really want to press this matter at this time?* Jesse responded:

*"Yes, I really do. It's happened many times before and I have always let the matter drop and behaved like a dutiful employee. I **need** to say something the next time this happens."*

Take a Stand

Even if you separate needs from wishes, you can't spend every waking hour clarifying all the important interpersonal issues that occur in your life. With so much going on, you probably tend to put things on hold. The danger, of course, is that you may never get back to them. As a result, things pile up and you never decide where you stand.

Think of three piles. The pile on the left includes behaviors you find acceptable. The pile on the right contains actions you find unacceptable. The pile in the middle is where you place matters you are unsure about.

acceptable

unsure

unacceptable

For most people, the *unsure* pile is very high, so much so that many items are buried and forgotten. Individuals who are people smart frequently do a spring cleaning. They sort through the pile and place as many items as possible in the *acceptable* or *unacceptable* piles. The rest of us keep piling on more issues.

To assert your needs, it is imperative that you review where you stand on the most important matters you face. You can't use the excuse that you are too busy. Imagine if you got clear about one issue every week of the year; by the end of the year, you would have taken a stand on 52 issues!

Of course, lots of situations are difficult and you might waffle about what stand to take. Remember that your positions do not have to be permanent. When you are really unsure what stand to take, experiment for a week with a particular position and see how it feels. Don't get frozen by indecisiveness. When you straddle the fence, you'll never learn where you want to stand. Don't worry if you decide to change your mind. Others will see you as thoughtful rather than indecisive.

It is especially helpful to take a stand first on matters where people want something from you rather than the other way around. That's because you have far more power to say "No" to someone's request than to make a successful request of others. Write down a list of possible "no's" you would like to express:

When I Need to Say No

I would like to say no when:

1. _____
2. _____
3. _____
4. _____
5. _____
6. _____
7. _____
8. _____

Review this list and select a few to act on immediately, then move on to situations where you want to say to others, "Do this." Spend some time clarifying what you want others to do by focusing on two key questions:

- What specifically do I want to see changed?

- Am I willing to accept a partial change, or do I want the entire situation improved?

Jesse was asked these questions about her objection to starting a project and then being pulled off it into another assignment:

> *Interviewer: What specifically do you want to see changed?*
>
> *Jesse: I would like a week's notice before being given a new assignment.*
>
> *Interviewer: Are you willing to accept a partial change or do you want the entire situation improved?*
>
> *Jesse: Well, I guess I'm not in a position to insist on this advance notice. I would settle for this gesture: When my boss decides he needs me on another assignment before I have finished a previous one, I want him to give me the opportunity to discuss the situation first with him and see if there are other solutions rather than simply being told to quit what I'm doing in favor of something else. If it can't be helped, then I'll live with it.*

Communicate Your Position

Having clarified what you want, you are now ready to express your need to the other person. Don't beat around the bush. That makes others suspicious and defensive. Go through the front door instead of the back! Use phrases such as:

- I would appreciate it if you____(call me first thing in the morning).

- I will not____(be able to come to the meeting).

- It would be great if you____(could give me a day's notice).

- I will have to____(turn down your request).

- Please____(tell me when you are taking the car).

- I would prefer that you____(get assistance from someone with more free time).

- It works best for me if____(you put it in writing).

- I've decided not to____(volunteer this time).

Avoid questions such as, "How about a thank you?" or, "Don't you think you could knock first?" Rhetorical appeals almost never get results. To help you avoid them, focus on what you want from the other person whenever he or she is doing something that interferes with your needs. Often, there is a tendency to comment on the person's behavior instead. A comment such as, "You're being a nag," for example, is far less direct than a statement such as, "I'd like you to tell me just once when you want me to do something for you." Commenting on other people's behavior often happens because we are uncomfortable about owning up to our feelings of anger. Instead of talking directly about our anger, we often cover it by accusing someone. For example:

Assume it's Sunday and a brother and sister, Joel and Debby, are playing so noisily that they wake their baby sister in the middle of her daily nap. They know how important it is to be quiet in the vicinity of the baby's room, but lately they have been quite forgetful about this. Their father, Marty, is livid and yells, "How many times do you need to be told to keep quiet during the baby's nap? You're both totally inconsiderate." Marty would have been better off saying more directly, "Now the baby is awake, my afternoon is loused up, and I really resent it."

In some cases, you may feel that it is important to convey some sensitivity to the other person while still standing up for your needs. You can accomplish this by adding some recognition of the other person's situation as in, "I realize you have been really busy, but I want you to make time for me." On the other hand, you may want to convey firmness if your prior assertive statements have been rejected. It may even include the mention of some type of consequence as in, "I am warning you that I will take this matter to Human Resources if we can't resolve it ourselves."

2. Remaining Calm and Confident

No matter how direct and straightforward you are about your needs and requests, there is no guarantee they will be honored. Communication is a two-way street. You will get a response, but it may be one you will not like. Being truly successful in meeting your needs is a result of how you react to unfavorable responses. You can undo all your hard work in expressing yourself directly at the beginning of the encounter if you become frustrated or angry in the middle of it. The key is to stay calm and confident in the face of resistance.

The problem is that few people can calm down just by being told to do so, or even by making their own personal resolution to relax. It takes a lot more. While there is no complete cure for over-reaction, there are three steps you can take to remain calm and confident under fire: *stay on track, give reasons nondefensively,* and *watch your body language.*

Stay on Track

As soon as you get any resistance to your request, the smart thing to do is to ask yourself: *What is my goal?* This action works like a circuit breaker so that you do not blow a fuse. It keeps you focused on what you want to accomplish rather than setting off your emotions:

> *Sandy just finished giving a report to his team about how to improve the company's website. He worked long and hard on this report and was pleased with the quality of his recommendations. He was eager to find out how others felt. Rather than receiving kudos for his report, all he got was nitpicking. Showing his annoyance, he then said: "I would really appreciate it if you would discuss the value of my core recommendations and not get bogged down in little details." A teammate retorted: "Sandy, don't get so uptight. Aren't you open to feedback?" When he heard this remark, Sandy was about to lose control but he remembered to say to himself: "What's my goal?" Steadying himself, he calmly replied: "I do want your feedback, but it needs to focus on my core recommendations to be helpful to me and the team at this juncture."*

Notice that Sandy essentially restated his needs rather than react to his teammate's remarks. People can get us off the topic by saying things to divert us or by sulking or acting miffed. One of the best ways to fend off the first maneuver is to calmly repeat what you want. Another strategy to add to your arsenal is a quick response to people's protests, such as "that may be," "that's not what we're talking about," or "Maybe, I am (stubborn, uptight, etc) but____" When resistance is silent, the best thing to do is ask a question, such as: "Tell me what you're thinking."

Finally, don't be afraid to say things such as, "Let me think about it for a few minutes," when you feel pressured to do something you would rather not do. Enjoy the pause that refreshes. People often have the notion that they have to respond instantly to other people's requests. Saying no gracefully and with tact comes easier if you take your time to clarify thoughts and decisions, especially when you're unsure where you stand or you've given a quick response under pressure and would like to rethink matters. If your eventual decision turns out to be unpopular with the other person, so be it.

Give Reasons Nondefensively

Often asserting your needs requires an explanation. The key is to explain yourself so that you are informative, without being defensive. Give a brief, respectful, honest explanation for your position as in, "I don't want to go out for dinner because I think we need to watch our spending right now." Too often, however, people go on and on as if their position were not justifiable until others agree with them (something they seldom do).

If you stop rather than go on and on, you give breathing room for the other person to reply and even to object. Don't be concerned about that. You can't filibuster forever. Giving room for a response shows your confidence that you can handle whatever happens. Notice in the following example how Ray holds the line with regard to his position about dinner and takes the knocks along the way:

Ray: I just think we can't handle that expense right now.

Chris: You always say that when it's something important to me, but if it's important to you, you somehow find the money!

Ray: That may be. I know I can be inconsistent, but right now, I don't think we can afford it.

Chris: Stop wiggling out of this one. You drive me crazy with your righteous attitude.

Ray: I'm sorry you feel that way, but I think we should not do this.

Chris: You can be so stubborn.

Ray: You're right about that.

It's also smart not to offer too many apologies. Being overly apologetic leaves the impression that you are guilt-ridden and uncertain. You might even say, "I wish we could see eye to eye, but unless we come up with a novel solution or great compromise, I am not prepared to change my stance." Sometimes a simple, "I'm sorry" without further defensive talk is the best course of action.

Watch Your Body Language

People pick up subtle cues in your body language that suggest that they can get the upper hand. Doreen goes to Jim's office and says to him:

"Jim, I've been meaning to talk to you about the off-color jokes you tell around the office. They make me uncomfortable." As she says this, her eyes look away nervously, her voice quivers, and her body is cringing. She realizes this, but hopes her fragility will bring a sympathetic response. However, Jim says: "Doreen, I didn't know you were so upset about the jokes. But why are you picking on me? All the men around here do it. No big deal."

Doreen feels defensive and she shows it by saying, in a soft, halting tone, "I . . . I don't want you to be upset, really I don't. OK? I'm talking to you because you tell more off-color jokes than anyone else. At least, that's the way it seems to me." Sensing that Doreen is serious but still uncomfortable, Jim replies: "I didn't know you felt that way. I'll try to knock it off." Doreen accepts Jim's half-hearted commitment with a weak smile and leaves his office.

Tone of voice, gestures, and eye contact greatly affect the way another person decides how insistent you are—no matter how carefully you select your words. Work at improving your assertive body language and voice tone by looking over the chart below and selecting areas where you need improvement.

Vocal Nonverbal Behavior		
Nonassertive	*Assertive*	*Aggressive*
voice too soft	moderate loudness	voice louder than needed
frequent pauses	even, fluent speech	fast speech
questions	declarative sentences	exclamatory sentences
Facial Nonverbal Behavior		
Nonassertive	*Assertive*	*Aggressive*
little eye contact	open, direct contact	glaring, staring
tense facial muscles	relaxed, friendly	tense facial muscles
(fear)		(anger)
pleading, timid look	confident, engaged look	impassive, stony look
Postural Nonverbal Behavior		
Nonassertive	*Assertive*	*Aggressive*
fidgeting, wringing hands	open hands	clenched fists
hands behind back or in pockets	hands at side	finger pointing
nervous, shifting body	relaxed body position	rigid body position

3. Being Persistent

We all face situations in which problems persist even though we have been very clear and firm about our expectations. We thought that a matter was settled, only to find that the other person continues doing something we find unacceptable. Many people get discouraged when this happens and abandon their efforts to obtain a change in behavior, or they postpone them until another time. As a result, they let the person off the hook.

The key to getting a lasting solution is persistence. When you are persistent, you send the message that you are really serious. If the other person has never experienced your persistence before, he or she is apt to slack off.

Persistence does not mean nagging. Nagging is usually an expression of frustration rather than confidence. The person who persists is in control rather than out of control.

Three techniques are worth considering to be persistent in your efforts to inspire change: *reminding, requesting*, and *encouraging*.

Remind

Although you have asserted yourself until you're blue in the face, the other person may continue to behave as before. One option is to remind the person frequently what behavior is acceptable and what is not, until change occurs. Through repetition of your expectations, the other person learns that you will persist regardless of his or her forgetfulness or attempts to discourage you.

There are three key elements in using reminding as an option:

1. Select a specific behavior you'd like to change, such as keeping the family room tidy or getting to the meeting on time.

2. Communicate your expectation on a regular basis: Don't wait for infractions to occur.

3. Avoid other remarks and criticism. Give the plan a week. Express appreciation for any encouraging efforts during the week.

You can state your expectation verbally or in writing. If you verbalize your reminder, keep it simple and brief. For example, you might say: "Please remember to_____" or "I'm counting on you to_____" If you feel like a nag, try leaving written messages or creating a small sign. A short note that says, "REMINDER:_____" can be very effective.

Reminding is a slow but steady method. Its success depends on systematic, quiet repetition. Some people resist using this approach by claiming, "She should know what she's supposed to do." That may be true, but she may not know how serious you are about the matter. Repeated reminders, not done in the spirit of nagging, can convey your determination.

Request

It's amazing how often people assume that undesirable behaviors can be changed only if they tell the other person what has to happen. Requesting involves asking, not telling. Rather than setting down the law yourself, you can use the alternative of bringing your concerns to the other person and requesting him or her to work out a plan for altering the problem. You can demonstrate confidence when doing this procedure by approaching the other person with the attitude that you expect a serious consideration of your needs.

When you use this approach, take the following two steps:

1. State what the other person is doing that is unacceptable to you: "You still leave the kitchen a mess," or "You still give me last minute assignments."

2. Ask: "Are you willing to talk about changing this situation?" If the answer is yes, don't rush into giving advice. Instead ask, "What would you be willing to do about it?"

If the person makes an acceptable offer, respond with words like, "I appreciate your promise and I am counting on you to keep it." More than likely, you will get a vague promise to change. Accept it, but also press for a more specific commitment. If the person wants to strike a bargain with you, you have the option to accept or refuse. If the person dismisses your invitation with a shrug, try repeating yourself: "No, I really mean it. Are you willing to_____?" If you still get nowhere, then make a request to think over the conversation and return to the discussion at a time you think appropriate. Be persistent. Don't let one attempt at this strategy suffice.

Naturally, any commitment you obtain needs to be monitored. Be persistent about keeping the person to his or her promise.

Encourage

Encouraging is a plan to promote positive behaviors by complimenting any actions that are steps toward the desired results. Often, when a person is not behaving as we'd hoped, the usual response is to bear down on the failures. If you look hard enough, you can notice positive signs that, if nurtured, will bring about the overall result you are seeking.

The key to this approach is to eliminate any criticism for awhile. Persist with positive messages only. For example, you might note and reinforce the following:

- an occasional attempt to keep a room tidy

- a better than usual report from a member of your staff

- a willingness to assist you in a chore

- an attempt at friendliness

- taking initiative

- handling something instead of asking you to do it

Don't defeat your own purposes by giving exaggerated praise. People don't believe overly effusive compliments. They may also feel manipulated. Straightforward, no-fuss messages produce the best results: "That was better." "Nice going." "Thanks." Remember to keep a positive focus for at least a week to demonstrate your sincerity and persistence.

Try It
Exercises for Developing Your Assertiveness

Armed with some motivation and tips, it's time to try it out. Here are some experiments you can undertake right away to work on your goals and find out if you like the results:

Being Decisive

1. Make a list of requests people make of you that are a burden. Review the list and select one or two requests that you will refuse in the next week. Think about how you will politely, but firmly, inform someone of your need to say "no," then carry out your plan.

   What happened? Did you feel less guilty than you thought you would?

2. Review the requests you want to make of others to help you meet your own needs. Select one or two. Get clear in your mind what you specifically want. Formulate each request so that it is as reasonable as possible for the person you will ask, then make your request(s).

Did you get a positive response? Are you happy with the support you obtained?

Remaining Calm and Confident

1. Work on staying calm and confident in situations that usually cause you stress. Plan in advance how you might handle these situations in order to feel more confident. When the situation occurs, take a deep breath, slow yourself down, and talk just enough to express your wishes. Don't get defensive or caught up in power struggles or blow your cool. If you lose control of your emotions, recognize when it is happening and gain a grip on yourself.

What were the results? Do you like how you handled yourself?

2. Take one of the following strategies and practice it for one week with a variety of people and in a variety of situations. Work on it until it becomes second-nature.

   • Repeat yourself rather than respond to someone's remarks.

   • Avoid arguments with others by using phrases such as, "That may be," "We see it differently," and "That's true, and_____"

   • Give brief, non-apologetic explanations for your position.

Being Persistent

1. Work on your persistence. Identify times when you give up too easily or flip-flop on an issue on a day to day basis. Make a small list of decisions you would like to stick to in the coming week. After the week is up, look over your list and give yourself a grade: A=stuck to my guns; B=persisted most of the time; C=persisted some of the time; D=gave up.

2. Select one of the three creative options for persisting (*reminding, requesting, encouraging*), and try it for one week with someone who might benefit from it.

Live It
Overcoming Your Own Barriers
to Lasting Change

As you attempt to develop your assertiveness, you should expect that the road ahead will be full of personal land mines. As you navigate this road, be aware of those factors that have prevented you in the past from acting assertively. Here are some obstacles most of us have to overcome to create lasting change; use our prescriptions to help yourself move forward:

I am afraid that I will offend someone or hurt his or her feelings.

> Think about whether you are taking on the responsibility for the other person's feelings. You have not signed a contract that says you must protect others from feeling upset. There is no way of handling all situations so that nobody feels badly. Ask yourself: "What will be the long-term effects on this relationship, on the other person, and on myself if I don't say what I want, feel, or believe? Will these long-term effects be worse than the short-term discomfort I or the other person may feel if I am assertive now?

I want to be accepted.

> When you appease someone, you don't win acceptance; you give that person encouragement to push you around again. Continual non-assertion erodes your sense of self-acceptance and in some cases leads to a general sense of worthlessness.

I can't help getting into power struggles and arguments with certain people.

> As you wait for these people to stop being argumentative, they are waiting for you to stop as well. Make the first move!

Even if you feel that the other person is extremely difficult, you can decide not to argue. Express your needs. Give brief, nondefensive reasons for them. End the conversation before it turns into a full-blown argument by saying, "Please think it over."

I am unsure if I have a right to say "no."

Sometimes, it's difficult to make this determination. But, if you continue to err on the side of caution, you will never find out if saying "no" is the best decision for you and possibly for the other person. The test question to apply is, "Will saying "no" help me to be more effective?"

I have a bad temper and lose hold of my emotions too quickly.

Slow down in the middle of a confrontation by taking a few breaths and doing a goal check (What is my goal right now?). You might want to say to the other person, "Can we start over again? I feel like things are getting out of control."

I am just not very decisive.

Making no decision is often worse than making the wrong decision. We learn something from trying out decisions— even poor ones. Remember that you do not have to make permanent commitments to a course of action. Try it for a week and see if you like the results. If not, reverse gears. Take prudent risks and evaluate the outcome.

I take a stand, get the result I want, but eventually the person goes right back to the same old behavior.

It is hard to be persistent. Review the three options, remind, request, and encourage on pages 22–24.

With some people, I don't know where to begin. They do so many things that drive me crazy.

> The key is to start somewhere specific. Give yourself a week to work on one matter at a time. Once you get compliance in one area, it becomes easier and faster to get other issues resolved to your satisfaction.

Don't give up on yourself. When you experience the occasional setback, remind yourself to take it a day at a time. It's the only way to go the distance!

Putting It All Together

In the Introduction to this booklet, we promised a realistic five-step development plan. After reading page after page of advice, checklists, and exercises, however, you may feel a bit overwhelmed. We'd like to put the whole back together again by giving you a short review.

Asserting Your Needs

When they need to set limits or advocate for themselves, people smart individuals:

Are decisive by:

separating needs from wishes

taking a stand

communicating their position

Remain calm and confident by:

staying on track

giving reasons nondefensively

watching their body language

Are persistent by:

reminding

requesting

encouraging

Schedule specific dates to start using the skills you've decided to try out. Decide on ways to monitor and evaluate your progress by getting feedback, keeping logs, or retaking the self-test at regular intervals. The following steps provide a framework to guide your efforts. Fill in the blanks to create your personalized change plan.

My strengths are: _____

_____

_____

_____

_____

_____

_____

The areas in which I most want to improve are: _____

_____

_____

_____

_____

_____

_____

_____

The specific skills I need to work on to improve in these areas are:

_____

_____

_____

_____

_____

_____

_____

_____

_____

The key situations in which to use these skills more effectively are:

_____

_____

_____

_____

_____

_____

_____

I intend to do the following practice exercises to enhance my skills:

_____

_____

_____

_____

_____

_____

_____

_____

The barriers I'm most likely to encounter are: _____

_____

_____

_____

_____

_____

_____

_____

The strategies I plan to use to overcome these barriers are: _____

_____

_____

_____

_____

_____

_____

_____

_____

My personal action plan is to begin using my target skills in my selected situations by _____*(supply date).*

In addition to creating your own action plan, make a copy of these reminders and post it where you will see it often.

Asserting Your Needs Reminders

- Be straightforward and direct.
- Get proactive rather than reactive.
- Don't get into power struggles.
- Stay focused on what you are trying to achieve.
- Don't overapologize and overjustify.
- Keep calm and remain confident under pressure.
- Say "no" when you need to.
- Speak up and don't be afraid to ask for things.
- Above all, be clear and decisive.

As you work on developing assertive skills, be patient with yourself. As Confucius once said, "It does not matter how slowly you go, so long as you do not stop." We promise you that the investment will be worth it.

References

Covey, S. (1990) *The 7 Habits of Highly Effective People*. New York: Fireside (Simon & Schuster).

Fensterheim, H. and Baer, J. (1975) *Don't Say Yes When You Want to Say No*. New York: Dell Publishing.

Gardner, H. (1993) *Frames of Mind: The Theory of Multiple Intelligences (Tenth anniversary edition)*. New York: Basic Books.

Goleman, D. (1995) *Emotional Intelligence*. New York: Bantam Books.

Jakubowski, P. and Lange, A. (1978) *The Assertive Option*. Champaign, IL: Research Press.

Nirenberg, J. (1963) *Getting Through to People*. Englewood Cliffs, NJ: Prentice Hall.

Silberman, M. and Wheelan, S. (1981) *How to Discipline Without Feeling Guilty*. Champaign, IL: Research Press.

Toropov, B. (1997) *The Art and Skill of Dealing With People*. Paramus, NJ: Prentice Hall.

Wall, B. (1999) *Working Relationships*. Palo Alto, CA: Davies-Black Publishing.

About the Authors

Mel Silberman, Ph.D.

Mel Silberman, Ph.D., is professor and coordinator of the Adult and Organizational Development Program at Temple University where he received the "Great Teacher" Award. He is also president of Active Training, a provider of cutting-edge business and personal development seminars based in Princeton, NJ.

A licensed psychologist, he specializes in training and development, marital and family health, performance improvement, and team building. Dr. Silberman has written a dozen best-selling books for parents, business people, educators, and trainers, including *Active Training, Active Learning, How to Discipline Without Feeling Guilty, Confident Parenting, 101 Ways to Make Meetings Active,* and *101 Ways to Make Training Active.* He is also editor of *The Team and Organization Development Sourcebook, The Training and Performance Sourcebook,* and *The Consultant's Toolkit.* Dr. Silberman is a widely sought-after speaker and seminar leader for educational, corporate, governmental, and human service organizations.

Freda Hansburg, Ph.D.

Freda Hansburg, Ph.D., is a psychologist and facilitator of change both for individuals and for organizations. She currently maintains a clinical practice with individuals and couples and directs the Technical Assistance Center, a consultation and training program at the University of Medicine and Dentistry of New Jersey. A popular trainer and conference presenter, Dr. Hansburg has provided consultation to numerous behavioral health and human service organizations, taught in university settings, and published professional and popular articles.